B IS FOR BEAR: BEARS FACTS FOR KIDS

SPEEDY
PUBLISHING

Speedy Publishing LLC
40 E. Main St. #1156
Newark, DE 19711
www.speedypublishing.com

Like human children, bear cubs are extremely playful.

Bears are
found on the
continents
of North
America,
South America,
Europe,
and Asia.

Bears are large mammals that eat mostly meat and fish, with the exception of panda bears which are herbivores and live also entirely on bamboo.

Bear cubs are born in litters of 1 to 3 and usually stay with their mothers for about 3 years.

Bears have excellent senses of smell, sight and hearing. They can run very fast and are also good at climbing and swimming.

Bears have
a large brain
and are one
of the more
intelligent
mammals.

Bears care
deeply
about family
members.
They will risk
their lives and
even fight
to the death
in order to
save a cub
or sibling
from danger.

Bears take
a long sleep
in the winter
similar to
hibernation.
They will sleep
in their dens
and a mother
bear will also
have her cubs
in a den.

Made in the USA
Middletown, DE
18 December 2023